CLIFF CLIMBERS

Anita Ganeri

Raintree

Chicago, Illinois

www.heinemannraintree.com
Visit our website to find out
more information about
Heinemann-Raintree books.

To order:

☎ Phone 888-454-2279
💻 Visit www.heinemannraintree.com
to browse our catalog and order online.

© 2012 Heinemann Library
an imprint of Capstone Global Library, LLC
Chicago, Illinois

Edited by Rebecca Rissman, Dan Nunn,
    and Sian Smith
Designed by Joanna Hinton Malivoire
Picture research by Elizabeth Alexander
Production by Victoria Fitzgerald
Originated by Capstone Global Library
Printed and bound in China by CTPS

15 14 13 12 11
10 9 8 7 6 5 4 3 2 1

**Library of Congress Cataloging-in-Publication
Data**
Ganeri, Anita, 1961-
   Cliff climbers / Anita Ganeri.
      p. cm.—(Landform adventurers)
   Includes bibliographical references and index.
   ISBN 978-1-4109-4138-1 (hb)—ISBN 978-1-4109-
4145-9 (pb) 1. Cliffs—Juvenile literature. 2. Mountains—
Juvenile literature. I. Title.
   GB512.G35 2012
   551.43—dc22   2010050061

Acknowledgments
We would like to thank the following for permission to
reproduce photographs: Alamy pp. 8 (© Nature Picture
Library), 15 (© LOOK Die Bildagentur der Fotografen
GmbH), 17 (© Michael Kemp), 24 (© Jeff Rotman), 26
(© Lynne Evans); Corbis pp. 4 (© Bob Krist), 7 (© Layne
Kennedy), 10 (© Louie Psihoyos), 13 (© Dewitt Jones),
18 (© Jim Richardson/National Geographic Society), 23
(© Keith Ladzinski/Aurora Photos), 28 (© Randy Faris),
29 (© Southern Stock Corp.); Photolibrary pp. 6 (Alan
Majchrowicz), 12 (Bill Stevenson), 19 (Martin Harvey),
20 (Gordon Wiltsie), 25 (Ken Usami), 27 (Tony Waltham/
Robert Harding Travel); Shutterstock pp. 5 (© Vixit), 11
(© Monkey Business Images), 14 (© Markus Gann), 16
main (© Joe Gough), 16 inset (© csp), 21 (© Vixit), 22 (©
Antoine Beyeler).

Cover photograph of a woman climber scaling the upper
part of the south ridge of Gimli, Valhalla Provincial Park,
British Columbia, Canada reproduced with permission of
Photolibrary (Steve Ogle/All Canada Photos).

Every effort has been made to contact copyright holders
of material reproduced in this book. Any omissions will
be rectified in subsequent printings if notice is given to
the publisher.

Disclaimer
All the Internet addresses (URLs) given in this book were
valid at the time of going to press. However, due to the
dynamic nature of the Internet, some addresses may
have changed, or sites may have changed or ceased to
exist since publication. While the author and publisher
regret any inconvenience this may cause readers, no
responsibility for any such changes can be accepted by
either the author or the publisher.

Some words are shown in bold, **like this.** You can find
out what they mean by looking in the glossary.

Contents

Cracking Cliffs

Cliffs are steep walls of rock. They can be hundreds of feet tall. They are found along coasts, in mountains, and even in outer space.

White Cliffs of Dover, England

Cliffs are amazing places to explore.
Are you ready to go cliff climbing?

Creating Cliffs

Cliffs are shaped by **erosion**. This is when the wind, waves, and rain wear away the rock. If the rock is hard, it can take a long time to wear away. If it is soft, it can wear away very quickly.

CLIFF FACT
Waves smash into cliffs with huge force, eating the bottom away.

Great Heights

Some cliffs are easy for scientists to get to. To reach other cliffs, they need to fly by helicopter or plane.

CLIFF FACT

The world's highest cliff is Great Trango in Pakistan. It is 4,396 feet high. This is about the same as three Willis Towers on top of each other!

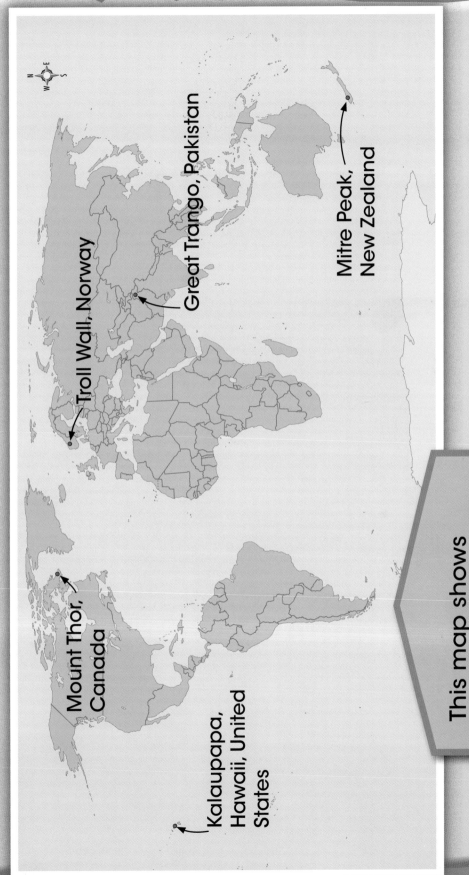

Troll Wall, Norway

Great Trango, Pakistan

Mitre Peak,
New Zealand

Mount Thor,
Canada

Kalaupapa,
Hawaii, United
States

This map shows
some of the highest
cliffs on Earth.

Cliff Climbers

Many different scientists study cliffs:
- **Geologists** study rocks.
- **Paleontologists** study **fossils** in rocks.
- **Biologists** study birds, plants, and animals that live on cliffs.
- **Glaciologists** study ice cliffs.

DANGER AHEAD!
Some people jump off cliffs for fun. This is called "tombstoning" because it is so dangerous. NEVER try this yourself.

Sea Cliffs

Some spectacular cliffs are found along coasts where waves wear rocks away. **Geologists** reach the rocks by climbing down the cliff face on a rope. This is called **abseiling**. They have to wear hard hats to protect their heads from rockfalls.

CLIFF FACT

The world's highest sea cliff is Kalaupapa, Hawaii, at 3,313 feet high. That's about the same as 11 football fields laid out end to end!

Kalaupapa, Hawaii

Cliff Features

The waves carve out different cliff features. Stacks are cliffs cut off from the mainland. Scientists climb up the rocks and **abseil** back down.

Twelve Apostles, Australia

stack

CAVE FACT
Sea caves were once used by **smugglers** to hide their loot.

Sea caves are holes in the bottom of cliffs. Scientists explore them by diving from boats.

Fossil Cliffs

The cliffs along the Jurassic Coast in southern England are 185 million years old. Here, **paleontologists** have discovered **fossils** of sea creatures, dinosaurs, and sea reptiles.

Jurassic Coast

Fossils like this can be found on the Jurassic Coast today.

pliosaur skull

CLIFF FACT

In 2009 scientists exploring the Jurassic Coast found the fossil skull of a pliosaur (sea reptile). It was over 8 feet long! That is nearly as wide as a bus.

Cliff-Top Colonies

Some cliffs are home to seabirds. Thousands of **gannets** nest on the cliffs of St. Kilda, off the coast of Scotland. **Biologists** have set up webcams on the cliffs, so they can study the birds without hurting or disturbing them.

gannet

albatross

CLIFF FACT

About half a million albatrosses **breed** on the cliffs of Steeple Jason, an island near South America.

19

Mountain Cliffs

Some of the tallest cliffs are on high mountains. Scientists can only reach them by climbing. They wear special clothes, boots, and helmets. They are joined together by ropes in case they fall.

CLIFF FACT

Some daring people climb cliffs without ropes. This is called free climbing, and it is very dangerous.

Ice Cliffs

Cliffs are not only made from rock. Huge ice cliffs tower along the coasts of Antarctica and on some mountains. To climb these cliffs, scientists wear special boots with spikes, called crampons, to help them grip the ice.

ice cliff

CLIFF FACT

If an ice cliff climber starts to slip, he or she digs an ice axe into the ice.

Cliffs Underwater

There are also cliffs to explore under the sea. They are found in deep-sea valleys, called **trenches**. To study them, scientists have to send down mini submarines, called **submersibles**. They use sound to make maps of the cliff features.

submersible

CLIFF FACT

The deepest undersea cliffs are in the Pacific Ocean. They drop about 5 miles. That is about the same as 1,500 giraffes on top of each other.

Crumbling Cliffs

All around the world, cliffs are collapsing into the sea. Scientists are trying to find ways to stop this. One way is to use rock armor. This means piling up boulders or chunks of concrete against the base of the cliff.

rock armor

Holderness coast

CLIFF FACT

About 2.2 million tons of the Holderness coast in northeast England crumble into the sea each year.

Becoming a Cliff Climber

If you want to become a cliff climber, you need to be good at science—and not afraid of heights! You may need to study a subject such as **geology** in college.

Being a cliff climber is an exciting career. Sometimes you might be based in a laboratory. You may also get to travel to cliffs all over the world!

Glossary

abseiling way of climbing down a steep cliff on a rope

biologist scientist who studies living things

breed to reproduce or have babies

erosion how rocks are worn away by wind and water

fossil remains of ancient plants or animals that have turned to stone

gannet large sea bird that lives and breeds in big groups

geologist scientist who studies Earth

geology study of rocks, minerals, and soil

glaciologist scientist who studies ice and glaciers

paleontologist scientist who studies fossils

smuggler person who secretly takes things to sell

submersible vehicle like a mini submarine, used for exploring the deep sea

trench deep valley under the sea

Find Out More

Find out

What is a fossil?

Books

Anderson, Sheila. *Landforms: Coasts*.
   Minneapolis: Lerner, 2008.

Claybourne, Anna. *100 Things You Should Know
   About Extreme Earth*. Broomall, Pa.: Mason Crest,
   2009.

Green, Jen. *Geography Wise: Coasts*.
   New York: PowerKids, 2011.

Websites

www.jurassiccoast.com
Hunt for fossils along the Jurassic Coast in the
United Kingdom.

**www.nps.gov/kala/naturescience/
naturalfeaturesandecosystems.htm**
Learn more about the beautiful cliffs of
Kalaupapa, Hawaii.

**http://kids.earth.nasa.gov/archive/career/
geologist.html**
Discover if a career as a geologist is right for you.

Index